SUMMER BADGE BOOK
de VERANO

Beanstack Badge Books
beanstack.com

TABLE OF CONTENTS
TABLA DE CONTENIDO

WELCOME
BIENVENIDOS

How To Use This Badge Book

This Badge Book works hand in hand with the Beanstack mobile and web apps.

Library and school users:
Download the mobile app or visit beanstack.com/find-a-site.

If you bought this book:
Download the mobile app and choose "On my own with Beanstack Go."

The app is the easy way to make sure you get credit for every minute you read.

1. Register or sign in to your free account.

2. Find the Summer Badge Book Reading Challenge in Discover/Challenges (mobile) or Challenges (web).

3. Tap the "Log Reading" button ("+" button in the mobile app) to start logging your reading and activities.

4. Scan the barcode of your latest book or type the title for instant logging.

Kids! Get help from a librarian or grown-up for this part.

 Questions? Visit badgebook.com/getstarted or check with your library or school. It only takes a minute or two to be up and reading!

¿Cómo usar el Badge Book?

Funciona en conjunto con las aplicaciones web y móviles de Beanstack.

Participantes de escuelas y bibliotecas:
Descarga la aplicación móvil o visita beanstack.com/find-a-site.

Si compraste este libro:
Descarga la aplicación móvil y selecciona "On my own with Beanstack Go."

¡Asegúrate de obtener crédito por cada minuto de lectura con la aplicación de Beanstack!

1. Inicia sesión en tu cuenta o regístrate para obtener una gratis.

2. Descubre el desafío de lectura del libro de insignias de verano accediendo a Discover/Challenges (móvil) o Challenges (web).

3. Selecciona el botón "Log Reading" en la web o el símbolo ➕ en la app para comenzar a registrar tu lectura y actividades.

4. Escanea el código de barras de tu libro más reciente o escribe el título para registrar tu lectura instantáneamente.

¡Niños/as! Pídanle ayuda a un familiar para esta parte.

¿Preguntas? Visita badgebook.com/getstarted o pregunta en tu biblioteca o escuela. ¡En solo unos minutos, podrás comenzar tu viaje de lectura de verano!

CALENDAR

1 **Write in the dates.**
Escribe los días del mes.

2 **Pop in a "Daily Reader" every day you read.**
Coloca un "Lector Diario" por cada día de lectura.

3 **Read a full row to earn a "Streak Week!"**
¡Lee todos los días para ganar una "Semana de Racha" Streak Week!

CALENDARIO

STICKERS

Unlock them all!

Complete the goals of your reading challenge.

Alcanza las metas del desafio de lectura.

Complete the pictures, games, and activities in the book.

Completa los dibujos, juegos y actividades en el libro.

Bonus stickers can only be earned on certain dates—so read often!

Solo podrás ganar las Extra calcomanías en fechas especiales, ¡así que lee consistentemente!

Don't forget your registration and completion stickers!

¡No olvides las calcomanías de registro y finalización!

¡Desbloquéalas todas!

CALCOMANÍAS

Draw yourself here

Dibújate aquí

My name / Me llamo: _____

READING PLEDGE
PROMESA DE LECTURA

⭐ **I am:**   **years old.**
Tengo: _____ años.

⭐ **I am going into:**   **grade.**
Estoy entrando a: _____ grado.

⭐ **My school or library's name is:**
El nombre de mi escuela o biblioteca es: _____

_____

⭐ **I like books about:**
Me gustan los libros de: _____

_____

I hereby pledge to read books that I love, all summer long!

Por la presente me comprometo a leer
los libros que amo, ¡durante todo el verano!

OFFICIAL SIGNATURE / FIRMA OFICIAL

CALENDAR LOG
CALENDARIO DE REGISTRO

MONTH / MES:

_____

SUNDAY DOMINGO	MONDAY LUNES	TUESDAY MARTES	WEDNESDAY MIÉRCOLES
☐	☐	☐	☐
☐	☐	☐	☐
☐	☐	☐	☐
☐	☐	☐	☐
☐	☐	☐	☐

THURSDAY JUEVES	FRIDAY VIERNES	SATURDAY SÁBADO	STREAK WEEK SEMANA DE RACHA
☐	☐	☐	
☐	☐	☐	
☐	☐	☐	
☐	☐	☐	
☐	☐	☐	

MONTH / MES:

_____

SUNDAY DOMINGO	MONDAY LUNES	TUESDAY MARTES	WEDNESDAY MIÉRCOLES
☐	☐	☐	☐
☐	☐	☐	☐
☐	☐	☐	☐
☐	☐	☐	☐
☐	☐	☐	☐

THURSDAY JUEVES	FRIDAY VIERNES	SATURDAY SÁBADO	STREAK WEEK SEMANA DE RACHA

MONTH / MES:

SUNDAY DOMINGO	MONDAY LUNES	TUESDAY MARTES	WEDNESDAY MIÉRCOLES

THURSDAY JUEVES	FRIDAY VIERNES	SATURDAY SÁBADO	STREAK WEEK SEMANA DE RACHA
☐	☐	☐	
☐	☐	☐	
☐	☐	☐	
☐	☐	☐	
☐	☐	☐	

MONTH / MES:

_____

SUNDAY DOMINGO	MONDAY LUNES	TUESDAY MARTES	WEDNESDAY MIÉRCOLES
☐	☐	☐	☐
☐	☐	☐	☐
☐	☐	☐	☐
☐	☐	☐	☐
☐	☐	☐	☐

THURSDAY JUEVES	FRIDAY VIERNES	SATURDAY SÁBADO	STREAK WEEK SEMANA DE RACHA

READING CHALLENGE
DESAFÍO DE LECTURA

SUMMER
Reading Challenge

Sign-up sticker

Calcomanía
de registración

Desafío de Lectura
VERANO

MY GOALS

Read this many books:

Leer esta cantidad de libros:

Daily reading minutes:

○ **20**   ○ **30**
○ **60**   ○ **___**

Minutos de lectura por día:

Book I'm excited to read:

_____
_____
_____
_____

Libro que me gustaría leer:

MIS METAS

Stick it!
¡Pégala aquí!

Date:
Fecha:

_____

How I earned this sticker:
Cómo gané esta calcomanía:

_____

_____

_____

_____

Date:
Fecha:

_____

How I earned this sticker:
Cómo gané esta calcomanía:

_____

_____

_____

_____

You got it!
¡Eso es!

REMEMBER: Log reading and activities through Beanstack to unlock the stickers!

RECUERDA: ¡Registra tu lectura a través de la aplicación de Beanstack para desbloquear las calcomanías!

Fill in this / Completa este
꠷ COMIC ꠷

MAZE / LABERINTO

Treasure hunters stole the Maya Codex of Mexico (an ancient book) and stashed it in their underground hideout! Can you get it safely back to the National Museum?

¡Unos cazadores de tesoros han robado el Códice Maya de México (un libro antiguo) y lo han ocultado en su escondite subterráneo! ¿Puedes devolverlo al Museo Nacional en buenas condiciones?

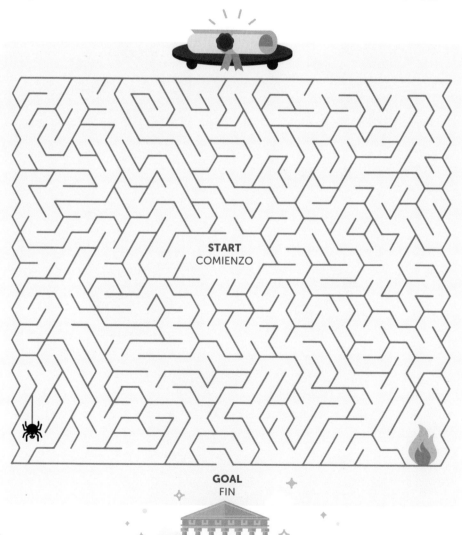

START
COMIENZO

GOAL
FIN

Date:
Fecha:

_____

How I earned this sticker:
Cómo gané esta calcomanía:

_____

_____

_____

_____

Stick it!
¡Pégala aquí!

Date:
Fecha:

_____

How I earned this sticker:
Cómo gané esta calcomanía:

_____

_____

_____

_____

You got it!
¡Eso es!

REMEMBER: Log reading and activities through Beanstack to unlock the stickers!
RECUERDA: ¡Registra tu lectura a través de la aplicación de Beanstack para desbloquear las calcomanías!

Date:
Fecha:

_____

How I earned this sticker:
Cómo gané esta calcomanía:

_____

_____

_____

_____

Stick it!
¡Pégala aquí!

Date:
Fecha:

_____

How I earned this sticker:
Cómo gané esta calcomanía:

_____

_____

_____

_____

You got it!
¡Eso es!

REMEMBER: Log reading and activities through Beanstack to unlock the stickers!
RECUERDA: ¡Registra tu lectura a través de la aplicación de Beanstack para desbloquear las calcomanías!

Your Majesty, people want to know more about you.
Describe yourself!

Su Majestad, la gente quiere saber más sobre usted.
¡Descríbase!

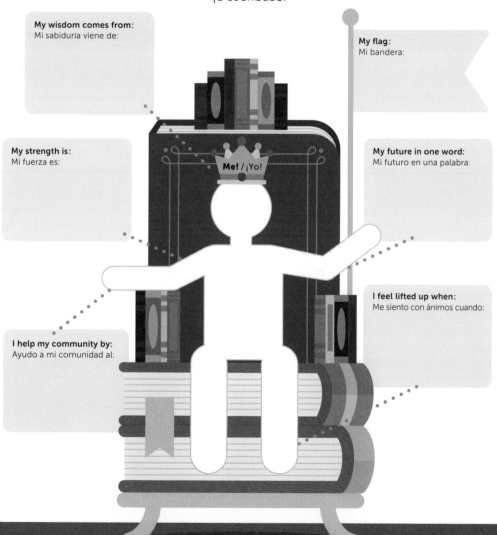

My wisdom comes from:
Mi sabiduría viene de:

My flag:
Mi bandera:

My strength is:
Mi fuerza es:

Me! / ¡Yo!

My future in one word:
Mi futuro en una palabra:

I feel lifted up when:
Me siento con ánimos cuando:

I help my community by:
Ayudo a mi comunidad al:

DESIGN / DISEÑO

The mayor wants you to invent the world's most amazing playground. Design it here!

La alcaldesa quiere que inventes el patio de juegos más asombroso del mundo. ¡Diséñalo aquí!

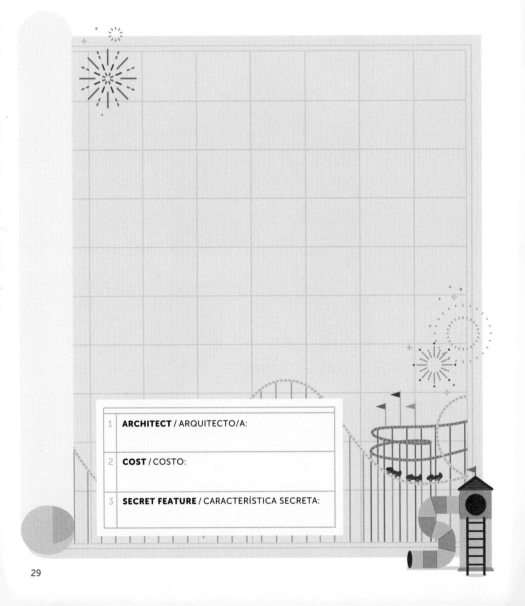

1	**ARCHITECT** / ARQUITECTO/A:
2	**COST** / COSTO:
3	**SECRET FEATURE** / CARACTERÍSTICA SECRETA:

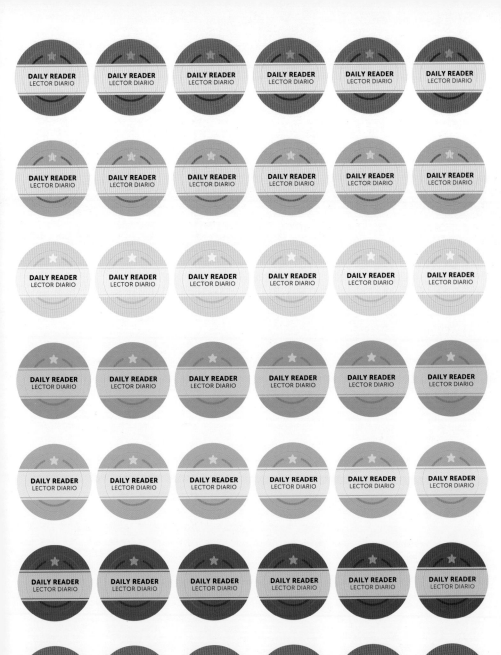

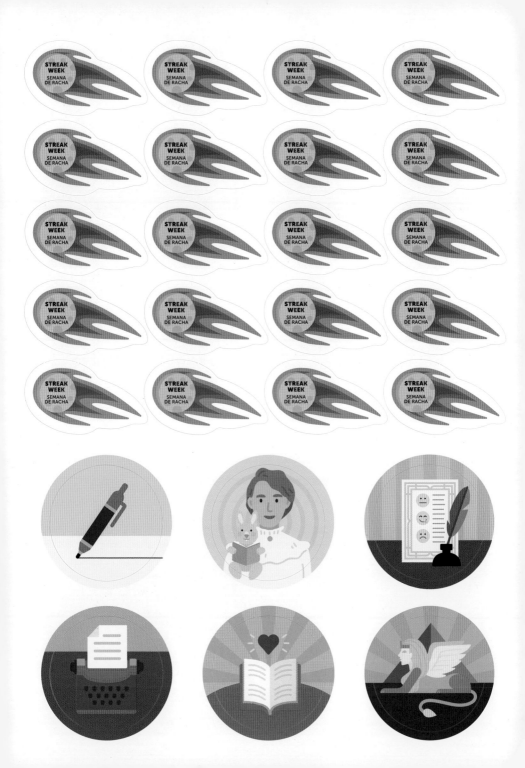

YOU'RE THE BEST!
¡ERES LO MEJOR!

DON'T STOP NOW!
¡NO TE RINDAS!

IMPRESSIVE!
¡IMPRESIONANTE!

OH YEAH!
¡MUY BIEN!

WAY TO GO!
¡ASÍ SE HACE!

SUPERSTAR!
¡SUPERESTRELLA!

KEEP IT UP!
¡SIGUE ASÍ!

SCORE!
¡GOOOOL!

LET'S GO!
¡SÍ SE PUEDE!

PRETTY GOOD!
¡ÉCHALE GANAS!

BIG CHEER!
¡FUERTE APLAUSO!

LOVE IT!
¡ME ENCANTA!

¡BRILLANTE!

¡FABULOSO!

¡FENOMENAL!

¡MAGNÍFICO!

PERFECT!

TREMENDOUS!

WOW!

¡SÚPER!

¡BRAVO!

FANTASTIC!

COOL!

EXCEPTIONAL!

GO!
¡VAMOS!

SUPERB SUMMER!
¡VERANO VICTORIOSO!

I DID IT!
¡LO HICE!

Stick it!
¡Pégala aquí!

Date:
Fecha:

How I earned this sticker:
Cómo gané esta calcomanía:

Date:
Fecha:

How I earned this sticker:
Cómo gané esta calcomanía:

You got it!
¡Eso es!

STICKERS
CALCOMANÍAS

CHALLENGE
(CONTINUED)

DESAFÍO
(CONTINUACIÓN)

Stick it!
¡Pégala aquí!

Date:
Fecha:

_____

How I earned this sticker:
Cómo gané esta calcomanía:

_____

_____

_____

_____

Date:
Fecha:

_____

How I earned this sticker:
Cómo gané esta calcomanía:

_____

_____

_____

_____

You got it!
¡Eso es!

REMEMBER: Log reading and activities through Beanstack to unlock the stickers!
RECUERDA: ¡Registra tu lectura a través de la aplicación de Beanstack para desbloquear las calcomanías!

CHARACTER / PERSONAJE

Create a hero card about a character from a book you've read!

¡Crea una tarjeta de superhéroe para un personaje del que hayas leído!

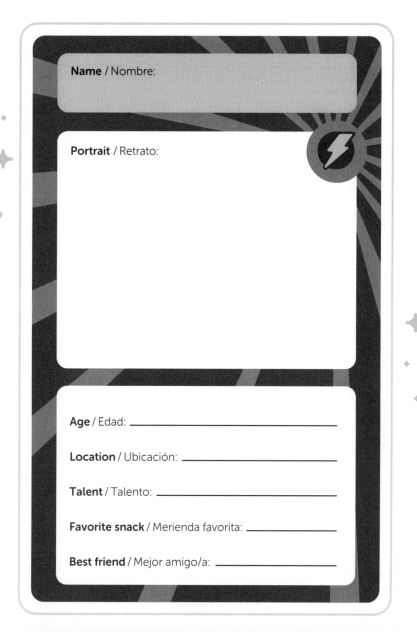

Name / Nombre:

Portrait / Retrato:

Age / Edad: _____

Location / Ubicación: _____

Talent / Talento: _____

Favorite snack / Merienda favorita: _____

Best friend / Mejor amigo/a: _____

Connect the missing pieces to their places!

¡Conecta las piezas para descubrir la imagen!

Tastiest snack while reading:
Bocadillo favorito mientras leo: _____

_____

Best bedtime book:
Mejor cuento antes de dormir: _____

_____

Favorite series:
Serie favorita: _____

_____

Good place to bring a book:
Lugar ideal para llevar un libro: _____

_____

Who reads the most in my home:
Quién lee más en mi hogar:

_____

_____

JUST FOR FUN! / ¡SOLO POR DIVERSIÓN!

**At the library, pick a book from the shelf
with your eyes closed!**

En la biblioteca, ¡elige un libro con los ojos cerrados!

Stick it!
¡Pégala aquí!

Date:
Fecha:

_____

How I earned this sticker:
Cómo gané esta calcomanía:

_____

_____

_____

_____

Date:
Fecha:

_____

How I earned this sticker:
Cómo gané esta calcomanía:

_____

_____

_____

_____

You got it!
¡Eso es!

What's happening below? Fill in the spaces.

¿Qué está sucediendo abajo? Llena los espacios.

Title of story / Título del cuento: _____

Tell your story to a friend! / ¡Comparte tu cuento con un amigo/a!

Can you fill in the missing drawings and numbers?

¿Puedes completar los dibujos y números que faltan?

1   **3** 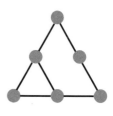 **6**

1   **4** 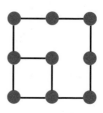 **9**

1   **5** 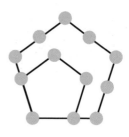 **12**

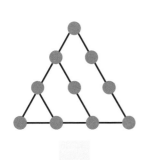

SUPER CHALLENGE!
¡SÚPER DESAFÍO!

What number comes next?
¿Qué número sigue?

16

These are tough!
¡Que complicado!

I've got this!
¡Puedo hacerlo!

40

Stick it!
¡Pégala aquí!

Date:
Fecha:

_____

How I earned this sticker:
Cómo gané esta calcomanía:

_____

_____

_____

_____

Date:
Fecha:

_____

How I earned this sticker:
Cómo gané esta calcomanía:

_____

_____

_____

_____

You got it!
¡Eso es!

REMEMBER: Log reading and activities through Beanstack to unlock the stickers!
RECUERDA: ¡Registra tu lectura a través de la aplicación de Beanstack para desbloquear las calcomanías!

Date:
Fecha:

How I earned this sticker:
Cómo gané esta calcomanía:

Stick it!
¡Pégala aquí!

Date:
Fecha:

How I earned this sticker:
Cómo gané esta calcomanía:

You got it!
¡Eso es!

Who is the best (or worst) villain from a book you've read?

¿Quién ha sido el mejor (o el peor) villano de un libro que hayas leído?

WANTED

REWARD
$ _____
RECOMPENSA

Name / Nombre: _____

Alias: _____

Crime / Crimen: _____

Worst trait / Peor rasgo: _____

Location / Ubicación: _____

SE BUSCA

Stick it!
¡Pégala aquí!

Date:
Fecha:

How I earned this sticker:
Cómo gané esta calcomanía:

Date:
Fecha:

How I earned this sticker:
Cómo gané esta calcomanía:

You got it!
¡Eso es!

Stick it!
¡Pégala aquí!

Date:
Fecha:

How I earned this sticker:
Cómo gané esta calcomanía:

Date:
Fecha:

How I earned this sticker:
Cómo gané esta calcomanía:

You got it!
¡Eso es!

You're a reporter! Interview an older family member.

¡Eres un/a reportero/a! Entrevista a un miembro de tu familia.

THE DAILY READER

EXTRA! EXTRA! READ ALL ABOUT IT

Grown-up's name:
Nombre: _____

Favorite book as a kid:
Libro favorito de la infancia: _____

_____

How many times they read it:
Cuantas veces lo leyó: _____

Why they loved it so much:
¿Por qué le gustaba tanto?: _____

_____

_____

¡ÚLTIMA HORA! ¡NO SE LO PIERDA!

EL LECTOR DIARIO

3 FAMOUS PEOPLE
I'd like to read about

Do you have a favorite singer? Athlete? Leader? Someone who inspires you? Jot down three names and visit your library to read about them!

¿Tienes un cantante favorito? ¿Atleta? ¿Líder? ¿Alguien que te inspire? ¡Escribe tres nombres y visita tu biblioteca para leer libros sobre ellos!

PABLO NERUDA
poet / poeta

1

BEATRIX POTTER
author / autora

MALALA YOUSAFZAI
activist / activista

2

DWAYNE JOHNSON
actor

CARLOS SANTANA
musician / músico

3

ALICE BALL
scientist / científica

3 PERSONAS FAMOSAS
de quien me gustaría leer

Date:
Fecha:

_____

How I earned this sticker:
Cómo gané esta calcomanía:

_____

_____

_____

_____

Stick it!
¡Pégala aquí!

Date:
Fecha:

_____

How I earned this sticker:
Cómo gané esta calcomanía:

_____

_____

_____

_____

You got it!
¡Eso es!

REMEMBER: Log reading and activities through Beanstack to unlock the stickers!
RECUERDA: ¡Registra tu lectura a través de la aplicación de Beanstack para desbloquear las calcomanías!

Stick it!
¡Pégala aquí!

Date:
Fecha:

_____

How I earned this sticker:
Cómo gané esta calcomanía:

_____

_____

_____

Date:
Fecha:

_____

How I earned this sticker:
Cómo gané esta calcomanía:

_____

_____

_____

_____

You got it!
¡Eso es!

BILINGUAL POP QUIZ

While you were reading this book in English, did you notice any of the Spanish along the way? See if you can connect the words below with their translations. It's ok to look back in the book for help!

Mientras leías este libro en español, ¿notaste el contenido en inglés? Pon a prueba tu conocimiento tratando de conectar las siguientes palabras con sus traducciones. ¡Puedes consultar las páginas anteriores si necesitas ayuda!

SUPERSTAR	BIBLIOTECA
PUZZLE	BIENVENIDO
SINGER	APLICACIÓN
SATURDAY	ROMPECABEZA
WELCOME	FAMOSO
STICKERS	LIBRO
APP	SUPERESTRELLA
LIBRARY	VERANO
BOOK	SABADO
FAMOUS	CANTANTE
SUMMER	CALCOMANÍAS

EXAMEN SORPRESA

HIGHLIGHTS AND FAVORITES!
¡DESTACADOS Y FAVORITOS!

Book I'd recommend to my friends:
Libro que le recomendaría a mis amigos/as: _____

_____

A new place I read about:
Un nuevo lugar sobre el que leí: _____

_____

Silliest character:
Personaje más gracioso: _____

_____

Best book cover:
Mejor portada de libro: _____

_____

Someone who reads with me:
Alguien que lee conmigo:

_____

_____

JUST FOR FUN! / ¡SOLO POR DIVERSIÓN!

Read a book outdoors!
¡Lee al aire libre!

**YAHOO! You just completed this season's challenge.
That's some serious brain exercise!**

¡YAHOO! Acabas de completar el desafío de esta temporada.
¡Este es un logro digno de admiración!

— CERTIFICATE OF —
COMPLETION
CERTIFICADO DE FINALIZACIÓN

CELEBRATE!
¡CELEBRA!

AWARDED TO: / OTORGADO A:

Name:
Nombre: _____

Date:
Fecha: _____

Number of badges earned:
Cantidad de insignias obtenidas: _____

Signature:
Firma: _____

EXTRAS

Wow! That much reading already?
¡Wow! ¿Tanto has leído?

One fact you learned about nature or history:
Un hecho que aprendiste sobre la naturaleza o la historia:

Most useful new word:
Nueva palabra más útil:

Check the Beanstack app to fill in these stats:

Accede a la aplicación de Beanstack
para completar esta información:

Longest book read:
Libro más largo leído:

Longest streak:
Racha más larga:

Most pages in a session:
Mayor cantidad de páginas leídas
durante una sesión:

Longest reading session:
Sesión de lectura más larga:

Check your Beanstack app and fill in your titles!

¡Visita la aplicación de Beanstack y registra tus libros!

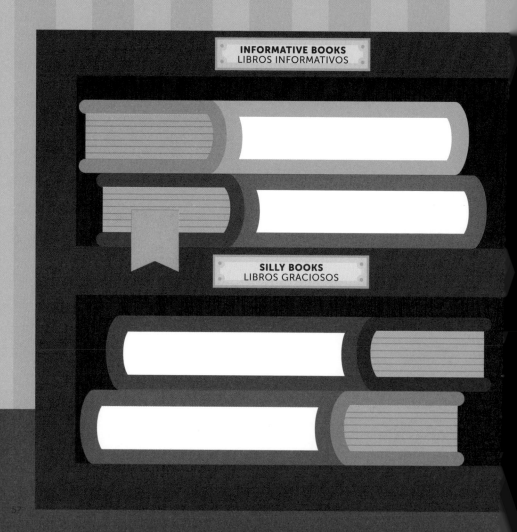

INFORMATIVE BOOKS
LIBROS INFORMATIVOS

SILLY BOOKS
LIBROS GRACIOSOS

THRILLING BOOKS
LIBROS EMOCIONANTES

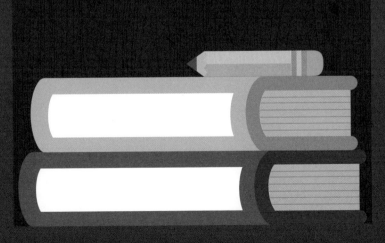

Total books read so far this year:
Cantidad de libros leídos en lo que va del año:

WOULD YOU RATHER

☐ **Spend the winter with a wolf pack in the Arctic?**
¿Pasar el invierno con una manada de lobos en el Ártico?

OR / O

☐ **Spend the summer exploring ruins in the jungle?**
¿Pasar el verano explorando ruinas antiguas en la jungla?

¿QUÉ PREFERIRÍAS?

Guest Book
Libro de invitados

Show off your reading! Ask your family, teachers, and friends to check out your Badge Book and leave a comment. You've earned it!

¡Presume tu lectura! Pídele a familiares, maestros y amigos que revisen tu Libro de Insignias y dejen un comentario. ¡Te lo mereces!

Name / Nombre:

Comments / Comentarios:

Name / Nombre:

Comments / Comentarios:

Name / Nombre:

Comments / Comentarios:

Name / Nombre:

Comments / Comentarios: